"All that we see or seem is nothing but
a dream within a dream."

-Edgar Allen Poe

For Mom, Dad, and Sean...thank you
for helping me realize my dreams...

-Maggie White

www.mascotbooks.com

A Christmas Guest

©2014 Maggie White. All Rights Reserved. No part of this publication may be reproduced, stored in a retrieval system or transmitted in any form by any means electronic, mechanical, or photocopying, recording or otherwise without the permission of the author.

For more information, please contact:
Mascot Books
560 Herndon Parkway #120
Herndon, VA 20170
info@mascotbooks.com

Library of Congress Control Number: 2014913512

CPSIA Code: PRT1114A
ISBN-13: 9781620867754

Printed in the United States

A Christmas Guest

Maggie White

illustrated by

Stuart Hausmann

I woke up from my nap,
Being only five,
To Mom buzzing in the kitchen
Like a bee in a hive.

"I forgot! I forgot!
Every cake must have flour!
Hurry, Jimmy! To the store we go.
It's Christmas. We can't spare an hour."

So off Mom and I flew
Out into the cold and snow.

Daddy grumbled a bit,
But warmed our car for us to go.

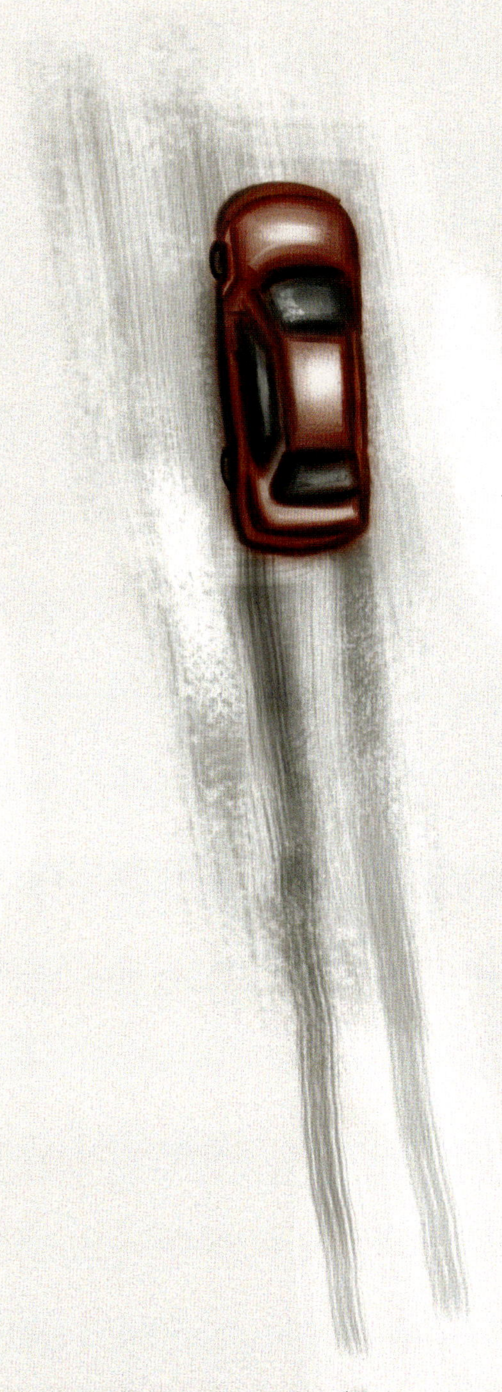

The streets were empty
But many windows were warmed and bright.
I heard laughing and music.
Couldn't wait for our Christmas party that night!

The store parking lot was empty.
I shivered. "Hurry, Mommy.
Daddy's waiting at home,
And my tummy's so hungry!"

On the way back,
I dreamed of cookies and cake.
I wanted my presents and treats
And all the food Mommy would make.

Then out the car window
I saw an old man in the street.
With long, dirty, white hair,
A scraggly beard, but no legs or feet.

Mommy saw him too
As other cars drove by.
He looked right at me
With one smiley blue eye.

"Mommy, stop!" I yelled.
"He's so cold and wet.
Can we take him home?"
She looked at me with regret.

Then she smiled at me,
Turning 'round so I could hear.
"You're right, honey!
Let's share our Christmas this year."

We stopped in the street.
Mommy helped him get in.
He didn't smell good at all,
But we shook hands and grinned.

He wasn't grouchy or scary.
He was a pretty funny guy.
He told me a special story
About a big star in the sky.

When we got back home
Into our nice, warm house,
Mommy looked at Daddy
Like the cat that swallowed the mouse.

Daddy shook his head and sighed,
Then looked at the old man and said,
"Sir, would you like some clothes and a shower?
Don't worry. You have nothing to dread."

Mommy went to finish dinner.
Dad said, "Stay here, kid."

I hoped the old man would have fun in the tub
Like I always did.

Before our dinner,
The old man wheeled his chair near me.
With Daddy's clothes and combed hair,
He was a nice sight to see.

Then we all sat down together
To begin our Christmas dinner.
With hands folded, the man's head bowed.
Somehow he looked smaller and thinner.

"Dear Father in Heaven," he said,
"Thank you for these dear friends tonight.
And help all those in the world
Who look at strangers with fright."

Mommy and Daddy smiled at each other.
We took hands and prayed.
We laughed and ate till our bellies were full.
The old man didn't go, but stayed.

He slept on our couch.
I let him hold my bear.
"Could you tell me if you see Santa tonight?"
He winked, "You'll know he's been here."

That night I dreamed about a baby
With angels singing, warmth, and light all around.
And to Him the animals bowed.
He smiled. I couldn't make a sound.

Then a gentle voice spoke in my ear
Like tiny bells I couldn't see,
"What you do for the least,
You do for Me."

I awoke so happy and light
For I knew my new friend was here.
"Merry Christmas!" I cheered,
As I ran down the stairs.

Presents from Santa filled the room.
Every size box under the tree.
But the room was too quiet.
My new friend, the old man, I didn't see.

Mommy and Daddy came in the room to marvel.
All the blankets folded, put back right.
They hugged me as I frowned.
"Jimmy, he must have left in the night."

"But, Mommy, Daddy, look!" I smiled.
A small golden box on an empty wheelchair.
"He left us a present."
We carefully opened it right there.

Now when I see a stranger, I smile.
My courage will rise.
Because the person you help
Could be the Lord in disguise.

The End

About the author

Born and raised on the south side of Chicago, Maggie White resides in Downers Grove, Illinois, with her husband, Sean and their five children, Colin, Moira, Shannon, Aileen, and Patrick. Maggie received a B.A. from Marquette University where she met her husband, and later went on to earn her M.A. in Education from Chicago State University. Besides her family, reading and writing has always been one of her greatest loves. Hopefully, the older the tribe of children gets, the more time she'll have to devote to books...perhaps it's not just wishful thinking!

Have a book idea?

Contact us at:

Mascot Books

560 Herndon Parkway

Suite 120

Herndon, VA

info@mascotbooks.com | www.mascotbooks.com